Trans Kung Fu: Awakening Self Acceptance

By Ashley Adamson

Legal

Trans Kung Fu: Awakening Self Acceptance by Ashley Adamson

Published by Ashley Adamson

978-1-4475-3999-5

Imprint: Lulu.com

http://www.AshleyxAdamson.com

Copyright © 2021 Ashley Adamson

Edited by Claire B. - Ashley's friend

Art + Cover by MelAr Buha

A note from the author

Wow you're reading this. I can't believe I finished. I've tried my best to condense this into the most important lessons learned on my trans journey of self-acceptance. There's a lot in here, and any paragraph could be expanded into an entire chapter or even it's own book. I will do that for another day. What you have here is a brief overview of something much deeper. I am hoping that if you do the work you will understand what I mean later.

If you want to get the most out of this guide, read slow, grab a journal, do the exercises, and meditate. Let your intuition and intent guide you. You will absorb what you need to know at any particular time, and I recommend revisiting this guide a few times as you transition.

I realized immediately after naming this book, that there needs to be a part 2 to focus on energetic systems, perception, and martial practice. If you join me for a live meditation sometime, I'll probably be teaching that too.

I have often described the process of writing this book to friends as a birthing process. This is my baby and last night I dreamt of giving birth. I have never dreamt like that. It's probably no coincidence that I also put the finishing touches on this book last night.

"Trans Kung Fu: Awakening Self Acceptance" is a symbolic commitment to embarking on a hero's journey and warrior's path. This is about self-love and self-acceptance. Remember: there is nothing to be destroyed; only to be transformed. But to transform you do need to break things. This gives space for them to return to their essence so that they may become fertile for transformation.

Framing this as Kung Fu reminds me of the intense work that needs to be done. Being a warrior on a path emboldens me to find inner strength to confront the things I am most afraid of and to keep pressing forward. It is my intent through this work that you find your strength and path on your journey. 🙏 - Ashley

What is Kung Fu?

What comes to mind when you hear the term? Martial arts? Fighting? I was no different growing up. My grandmother on my Chinese side would play show after show of Shaolin monks and mystical Princes and Princesses dancing in hand to hand combat.

It was not til much later when I began to transition that I truly understood the meaning of Kung Fu.

Kung Fu (功夫) is made of two characters. Kung (功), meaning effort or endeavor and Fu (夫), meaning time spent. Combined, this means the study and practice of something that requires effort and patience. In this sense anything can be Kung Fu, a pianist elevating their skills or a martial adept attaining black belt.

When thinking about one's transition it may often feel fluid, unstable, and a little unpredictable. Yet, there is a solidity to the process - you do make progress and as you come against your own inner walls you become more skillful at handling your battles with concepts such as dysphoria or the healthcare system.

When it comes to applying a framework for resilience, self motivation, and personal growth I cannot think of a better term to apply to one's endeavor on transitioning. There is nothing more transformational and life altering than to transition- it is a complete change inward and outward. And what you become after the process is nothing short of a miracle. For me personally, it has been deep awakening that has called into existence a new paradigm for my body and my spirit.

What if I were to say that you can become more powerful and adept at transitioning and facing your own inner demons? Would you believe me if I said you can surpass your own expectations?

The secret is in learning how to expand and contract. Let go and let in. When you realize that your main opponent is your identity then you can begin to unravel the process of attachment, burn it down, and begin the process of renewal and creation.

This guide is about empowering you with a story, a guide, and practices to unlock your highest potential form.

This is a book is about personal growth.

This book provides fundamental tools and concepts that will give you a framework for embodying self-acceptance, self-love, and ultimately be useful as a compass for navigating through the uncertainty in the best and worst of times. It's a short cut around mistakes through the 10,000+ hours I've invested in figuring out my transition and personal transformation.

This is for people who want a way to invest in themselves and have realized they are transgender. They want to get on the best track for realizing the greatest version of themselves the soonest!

Some of you have 100% committed to transition, others of you may be reading this as an exploratory exercise and some of you are in between and looking at the roadmap. Wherever you are, that's okay and you will benefit from reading this.

This is a resource that will help you throughout your transition. I suggest you bookmark and come back to revisit this as you grow and adapt. You may uncover deeper insights as your perspective changes. Share it with your friends - it will benefit them too.

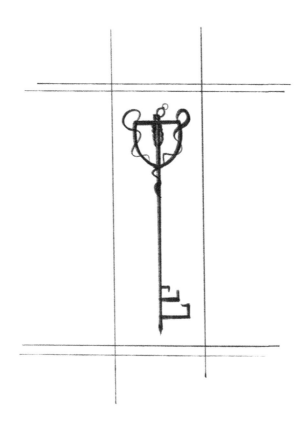

When you first realize that you are transgender there are probably a million thoughts racing through your mind. It's natural to begin searching the internet or elsewhere for information to provide a context for what you're experiencing. I've found a lot of the "how to" content for trans folks works on a narrow sliver of the problem of what it takes to transition. There are the obvious tangible things like "how to pass", surgery topics, and how to put on makeup and so on. And it makes sense, they're easy to google and recognize as "trans things." But I believe what's lacking is a more personal growth oriented guide that helps you with your journey through your transition.

You will find this guide goes much deeper than most as it will help you go within to find the key to unlocking your transformation from the inside out and the outside in.

My hope is this will have a lasting impact on your life through your transition and afterwards as these tools are broadly applicable to anything in life. If you'd like to go more in-depth with me you can come to one of my guided meditation groups or join a workshop I'll be hosting. More info on my website.

The transition

Nothing quite compares to a complete transformation. If anything, a gender transition will be the beginning of the greatest change of your life. A full metamorphosis from the inside out and the outside in. It's a special moment to cherish and while it can be incredibly tough at times when you make it out the other end you may see how much it was worth it.

A transition is a sacred and special process that few embark on. There is no right or wrong way to transition - with or without hormones; with or without surgery.

What even is a transition?

Conceptually, a transition is a process that occurs in a movement between two places - usually major. We often refer to a transition as it relates to letting go of something big, changing locations, changing jobs. In the case of you, this is about your gender.

If there's one thing all transitions take, it's time and effort. Your transgender transition is no different. As much as you and I would like to make the switch instantly, a gender transition isn't instant and can last for years if not decades.

Try to be patient with yourself as you go through this. No transitions are completely alike. Comparing will only make you feel like you're doing it worse. Give yourself a hug and then stick to your path ahead.

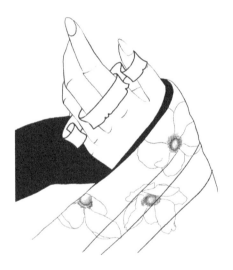

There's a lot of work to be done in a transition

Just like a role-playing game, transitioning transgender is a "choose your own adventure" with all kinds of sidequests you may want to take on as you build your character. And reading this guide will give you an XP boost like no other! 😆

A transition is not made up of one singular moment. It is made up of many small adjustments as you make changes and acclimate to those changes. It's often the little things that compound over time that make the biggest difference and ultimately take you to the end of your inevitable end of the transition.

When I started out I was overwhelmed at first with this massive to-do list that looked endless. It's easy to feel dazed by all the things to do. Be sure to give yourself time to figure out things.

A large part of transitioning is not the practical, easy to google stuff, but the rich universe of your inner world and how you can find the power to embrace change and love and accept yourself. We'll go into self-acceptance and your innerworld in more detail later, but first let's talk about the transition roadmap!

The transition roadmap

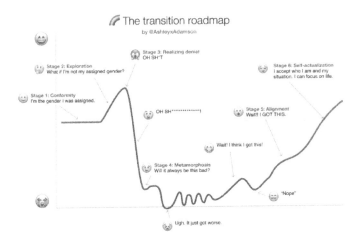

The transition roadmap
by @AshleyxAdamson

This is the transition roadmap which you may have completed already, are somewhere in between or maybe just getting started. Wherever you are this might shed some perspective and give you insight into yourself.

Having an idea of where you're at and also what's ahead might give you a better idea of framing your transition and also what challenges lay ahead. The most important thing is to understand it's a process and as you continue to take steps forward you will begin to see the light at the end of the tunnel.

I'll walk you through each major stage in the roadmap and then go into sharing my own personal story followed by a "thought meditation" which is to invite you to meditate on this thought, write in a journal or just thinking about it as you go throughout your day.

Stage 1: Conformity:

The first stage of a transition happens before you've realized you are trans. If you haven't figured out you're trans yet, you could be in this first stage.

For those who already have transitioned I think you will remember this phase.

Conformity means correspondence in form and appearance. Correspondence to who? To society, to your family, friends, everyone. We live in a world where most people still believe that assignment at birth equals gender. But for you maybe something begins to feel off. Why is it that you like things that are typical of another gender? Why is it that perhaps you desire to imagine yourself as another gender? At first, it is hard to know you're trans at this stage because you live in a world stuck to the script - birth sex equals gender. You have internalized that script. To make things more confusing, you aren't sure if this is just a phase you're going through or some other reason to escape something else.

Yet, slowly and incrementally you began to ask questions about yourself and society's expectations of you. This is the beginning stage where you realize you are conforming to something that is no longer in alignment with who you are.

Personal story:

Stuck in a cycle of self-repression. I escaped through computer games.

For me things started to feel off when I entered puberty. I remember spending time in the mirror looking into my eyes. "You would be so pretty as a woman." I would say. I secretly wished I could be, but shortly after thinking this I would repress the feeling and just shrug it off as "well I wasn't born a woman, that's how it works. So oh well. 🧕. This kind of "thought loop" of denial was based on the societal logic that birth sex equals gender. I kept in adherence with the gender paradigm I was born into and I didn't question it until much later.

Thought meditation:

Where have you felt that society has pressured you into thinking and adhering to your assigned gender?

If you're ready, it might be good to ask yourself:

- How can you experiment with your gender?

- What kind of tiny small things can you do right now for yourself to see what feels right? What comes up for you as you do this?

- Don't worry if it's difficult or doesn't make sense. A transition takes time.

Personal story:

The night I saw her for the first time.

In my late twenties, I finally worked up the courage to explore my gender. I had felt the desire to "crossdress" from childhood but always felt disgusting for liking it. The shame ran pretty deep and it took me years to get to a point where I could consciously give myself a chance to look past the shame. It was one fateful night when I went out clubbing with some girlfriends in my femme attire that I saw my feminine self in the mirror for the first time. I'll never forget the feeling. I was stunned to see someone else looking back at me. It was deeply moving and also incredibly euphoric. Was I really a woman? It felt like I had found a secret doorway into myself and now that I saw her in the mirror I didn't know if I could ever unsee that.

"Once you see,

you cannot unsee."

I was seeing the real me for the first time. In retrospect, this was my spirit guide showing me the power of seeing one's truth.

When you give yourself the gift to unbind your biased view of yourself you can get a glimpse of what's really there. I *really* was a woman. I had always been one. This was just the first time I could see. That vision will always remain burned into my memory. I couldn't accept it immediately. I tried to hide it from myself for several years which is the next stage in the roadmap - denial and realization.

Thought meditation:

Imagine yourself at the end of your life looking back on your journey.

- What did you most enjoy?

- What brought you happiness?

- What do you wish you would have done differently?

- Are there any regrets?

- What can you learn from this meditation to change your habits today?

Stage 3: Realizing denial

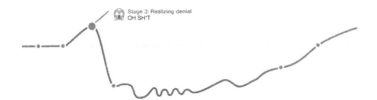

Okay! So when you enter or have entered this stage you have now seen enough to know you are not CIS and this is where climbing the next mountain begins.

"Never underestimate the power of denial."

Denial is a tricky feeling to uncover because its used by the mind to block out emotions and so in essence it feels emotionless. Which means if you try to find it by feeling for it you probably will not uncover it. Denial creates a void of no feelings. It hides them behind a hidden door. The good news is you have the key. You just have to find the key hole.

In the exploration stage you may have pursued uncovering your gender which will inevitably lead to a realization that a) you were in denial and b) you realize you are trans.

The logical mind can make up all kinds of stories here to keep you in denial.

Things like:

- "You're just pretending"

- "What if you're wrong?"

- "You'd never transition well."

- "You won't be accepted."

These kinds of thoughts keep us in denial because to confront these negative thoughts comes with a lot of baggage.

However, with enough exploration you will realize the true you. And when you do, you'll realize these negative thoughts are just what they are - thoughts. 🧘

Your moment of realization comes right after you realize you have been in denial. The realization of denial may be a singular moment, but more often it's a series of moments that keep recurring as a theme. This happened for me not only pre-transition but even while on hormones. I had doubt's even when on hormones but as I keep having more realizations I was able to shed the layers of self-doubt.

Personal story:

The day that I realized I was a woman thanks to the support of my friends.

Even after seeing my true self in the mirror it didn't change me enough to push me out of denial. In fact, I put more denial on the table by stopping dressing femme and slowly inching away from experimentation. I settled on being gender fluid and eventually non-binary as a safe alternative to admitting I was a woman because it had less risk and I didn't know for sure yet.

The thing that pushed me forward was a meditation where I looked back at my life - I have that meditation for you down below. I realized the path that I would have the greatest regret in not taking is not knowing 100% if I was a woman or not. With that, I decided "no regrets," I cannot live with a regret like that.

I pushed myself to experiment more and eventually after six months on HRT - yeah, SIX MONTHS on HRT 😆 my denial shell cracked. I had been dancing in femme presentation at Outside lands festival in San Francisco and was gendered as "she" by my friends.

Later, my partner asked me how it felt to be gendered "she" and that's when I realized it felt right. It felt SO right. This is when I had to tell my ego I had to admit I was wrong. I thought I had it figured out but actually something deeper inside already knew. I burst into tears at the realization that I was hiding from this fact of my own nature and that I had to accept I was a woman. This immediately carried with it all the baggage - as I saw it, of looking female and not passing and being ugly, which is how I've always seen myself. I was so afraid to be that "man in a dress," the objectified joke that I had unconsciously distanced myself from.

Thought meditation:

The best way to uncover your true self and get past denial is to follow your inner compass. If something feels right or it feels off, follow that feeling and see where it takes you. Listen to your intuition, it has a deeper "knowing" than your conscious mind.

Your denial hides your true self behind a door of repression. The door itself has no feeling, because that is the nature of denial - it is devoid of feeling.

The way to get around denial is to feel the feeling of yourself that already exists behind that door. The key is not to look for the door but look for the self behind the door.

- Close your eyes and take a moment to focus your attention within.

- Call out to what's on the other side.

- See what they say. If they could tell you something, what would they say to you?

"MARCO!"

"POLO!"

- Take a moment to listen.

More on denial and the inner compass when we get to the end of this guide.

Stage 4: Metamorphosis aka the trough

When you approach stage 4 you've now have acknowledged denial and are ready to move things forward. Good job! 🙌 Welcome to the best and worst stage of a transition! 😆 This is where reality sinks in and you begin the long journey of uncovering who you are and beginning to align that identity with the rest of the world.

It probably took years to get here. But now reality sinks in. What do you do now?

I remember at this stage I had the worst nights of crying myself to sleep and also the most euphoric moments of feeling completely merged with my spirit and feminine self.

This is the least stable part of your transition as anything can send you into a positive or negative spiral of emotions. This is also where gender euphoria usually hits frequently and hardest because you haven't normalized the validating experience of being your true self. This is also where dysphoria is usually the worst because you don't have strategies or a practice to cope with it.

Dysphoria about particular things can evolve over time as you transition. For me, I had no issues with not having breasts but as I chipped away at changing I eventually felt it was a necessity to get boobs.

In this stage, you'll feel the most "in transition" or in between at this point. You aren't solidly you yet. You're just figuring you out which makes it harder because you don't have a stable sense of self to fall back on. Although, this stage isn't all downs. Just be ready for when you do have your downer moments.

I also call the metamorphosis stage the "the trough" because this is where the long road to transitioning and stabilizing your identity is. While it's full of pure joy moments it's also the roughest. It gets better as you discover and align yourself but when you're in the thick of the journey it doesn't feel like there's an end to this stage. The key for me was to keep pressing forward. Whenever I would stop I could start to dwell on my problems and lose faith in my future. Avoid doing that. Keep going! 🏃,

The metamorphosis stage felt like I was changing my room - my room representing who I am. I had to get everything out of the room first then I could start painting it and figuring out what to keep, change, and get rid of. I felt like a constant mess inside but slowly I'd figure out where the major things in my room should be and from there it started to make sense.

The reason the metamorphosis stage can feel like it's a trough is multi-fold. Here's a few reasons:

- You lost confidence in knowing who you are since you just realized you aren't who you thought you are.

- You face all kinds of self-doubt, internal doubt, and external doubt from others.

- Your world hasn't aligned with your identity, you get misgendered, deadnamed, or mispronounced all the time now.

- You have to operate in a world that isn't supportive to being transgender.

- You haven't found your allies - a network and support system.

- You don't have strategies to mitigate problems brought up by healthcare, family, friends, work, and location.

- Life just overall feels like a mess because you haven't aligned it with your identity and you also don't know exactly who you are. So how can you align it?

- You don't know how to cope with dysphoria, so when it comes on it just beats you up inside.

Being in the trough sounds like a lot of pain - and it is but it's like anticipating a final exam versus taking it. If you come prepared it's a lot less worse than you imagine. That's why this guide is here to help you make it through your process more gracefully.

Let's also talk about the ups!

- You'll discover the beauty of who you are. It'll feel like a huge burden is lifted because you are no longer holding yourself back. A new version of yourself will emerge that feels more authentic.

- You'll experience life anew as if you were reborn again. This is one of the most astonishing things you can ever experience. A reset of your world while retaining the wisdom of your past self. It reinvigorated my wonder of what life can be. When you embrace who you are, suddenly the world can seem ripe with possibility.

- As you seek out community and friendship new people will emerge into your life that accept you and see you for who you are. While some friends may fade out, the new ones will come in. And who wants friends who conditionally like you for not being the true you anyways?

Note: This stage is very difficult at times. If you ever need immediate support, reach out to friends, family, or call the Trans Lifeline. It's not just for saving lives but also providing transgender resources and peer support. I've used it a few times when I felt really in the pits and lonely. I've also been an operator and can vouch for the integrity of the organization. They really *do* care and all of them are trans. It's completely anonymous. US (877) 565-8860 Canada (877) 330-6366

Personal story

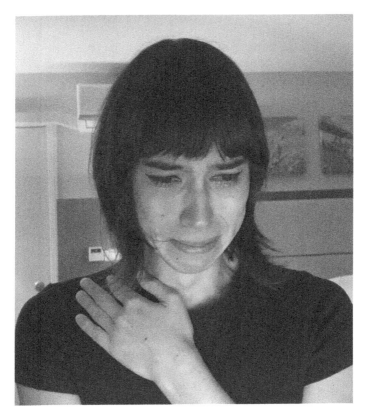

A moment of sharing my pain from my poem to "him."

My metamorphosis stage began when I accepted I was a trans woman - and it broke me. A wave of realizations washed over me. Suddenly, I could make all the connections to my past feelings of being out of place. Which also led me to come face to face with so many frightening prospects that I had stacked on the shelf of denial.

Would I be beautiful?

Would anyone see me authentically?

Would I be lovable to someone else?

Would I ever feel okay in my now grossly misaligned body?

"Why me? Is this my fate?" I said one late night alone in my airbnb rental. I was in a city I did not know on a retreat in Bucharest, Romania. The darkness of the church next to my window loomed over me like the sentinel of my new transgender identity. I felt so alone. Trapped.

I just remember crying into the infinite void. The tears kept coming and the darkness inside crushed me like a vice. I screamed out as if I were a child stuck in a well. I didn't know any other way to cope, it was one of my lowest points. I cried myself to sleep.

The only thing that got me through the darkest of times was realizing that there was more meaning to my life than just my experience alone. If I could learn something from the pain of this experience it's that I could take with me a gift to give to others and help them live a better life. This guide is one of those manifestations.

Thought meditation:

This part involves some deep work so take the time to make space to go into this one.

Start the process by doing some self care. Do something just for you that would be a meaningful symbolic gesture of love. Take the evening or full day or week to do this. Set the intent to be a loving gesture. This is important because you need to set a container of safety and set the undertone for when you enter the next phase.

The second phase of this process is then allowing yourself permission to experience your pain. Feel that thing that looms over you, feel the thing that feels uneasy inside you. Allow it to be born. Embrace it. Cry it out. Let the worst of it out in a loving and caring way. Allow your body to process. Find your heart and center your attention there. Let go of the mind and it's thoughts.

When I used to go through the pain I would allow my thoughts to say all kinds of horrible things to beat myself. Note: you should avoid using the mind in this situation but instead try to focus your attention on the feelings. They are just feelings and while valid are not always grounded in reality.

As these feelings come to the surface allow yourself to let them go and visualize yourself removing any parts of your identity that are attached to the feeling. By doing so, you are disconnecting your identity from the pain. That'll make it easier to let go. Your pain is not you.

As you stew in your feelings, begin to ask yourself for an anchor. Something that you can call upon to give you hope and meaning. What is it that you can gain from this? Where is the gift? Where is the growth? How can you make meaning out of this so you can move on?

Honestly, this is probably the hardest exercise. I wouldn't tread lightly here. I will have guided meditations and workshop offerings that I'll be announcing in my newsletter soon.

Stage 5: Alignment

As you adjust to the new conditions of your new self you will continue to experiment with seeing how things fit together in ways that make you happier. With a refined core and sense of being that has been through trials by fire you will find new more effective and powerful ways to recast the mold of your being into who you are and what you believe you are capable of.

In other words, if the previous stage felt like your room was a mess this is where you redecorate. You figure out where things go.

These are some of the questions you'll be asking and will have at least some answers to:

- What about your old self feels inauthentic?

- What new ways of being and expressing feel right?

- What things from the past do you want to keep?

- What things from the past do you want to throw out?

- Who are the friends that are your real supporters? Who are the fake ones?

- Who do you want to become?

At this stage you can confidently say you've created change in yourself and your world to align with your identity. This sense of alignment brings ease and more stability into your life and while it's not smooth sailing yet, it's far less a roller coaster and more like an unpaved road. You will still have the emotional bumps but it's not so extreme. The alignment stage is the slower gradual transition of the movement out of the trough.

Personal story:

I gained the courage to speak at my first conferance.

This stage felt like a slow build in retrospect. I had experienced a lot of the major transformations so I wasn't sure what to expect next. What I got felt like putting the finishing touches on my broad strokes of work. I had changed my name to Ash earlier and at the two year stage I changed it to Ashley. The name change was a symbolic commitment to move past my last marker of my non-binary past and embrace my own femininity.

There were lots of little moments that created alignment, like adjusting my thoughts as well as big life changes like moving cities. This is where I began to start sharing my voice on social media. I still wanted to give up at times but it took less energy to get back up and I became more confident in myself.

Thought meditation:

In the alignment stage you may feel like you are past something and then it'll reappear again and again. This is the part of the process where you finish peeling back the layers of the onion.

- At this point it's a good moment to reflect on these layers that you continually cycle back to and ask yourself what can you learn from your experience with them so far?

- Where is the remaining growth to be had to peel back more of the layers?

- Also, how can you let these problems retire? What does moving on from these problems mean to you?

- Are you attached or identified with them?

- What new narratives can you write for yourself here?

I talk about this in the tipping point video where the continual unraveling eventually leads to an inevitable resolution that sometimes you don't even notice. You can make progress here - there is an end to some of the challenges you may see as recurring themes in your reality.

Stage 6: Self-actualization

Self-actualization is the gift of putting in the time and effort to go into the depths of one's self and finding out who you are. Most people avoid this and somehow you have gotten through it. You are a miracle.

It has been a long journey. It's been the best and probably hardest thing you've ever done for yourself personally. You have gazed into the void, become accustomed to living in the unknown, and moved through high highs and low lows. Phew! That was tough. But now you have been forged in the fires and as a result you know yourself better than most people do. Congrats to you! You are becoming who you have always been. This is the long tail of the transition where subtle tweaks are made internally and externally. This is where you really settle into your gender and expression.

At this stage you accept who you are and where you're at in life. Sure, things are not perfect and perhaps there are still changes you want to make but overall you no longer struggle with your gender.

Things on your transition wishlist are checkboxes rather than big question marks about your identity. There's still plenty of things to discover about yourself but the internal war over your identity feels over. There may be an occasional hiccup now and then, but nothing new here - you know how to handle it. You are embracing the real you.

Personal story:

Left 2016: Shy enby confused, yet euphoric. Right 2021: Empowered, actualized, Ashley.

I recently visited a friend who hadn't seen me since I was 6 months HRT and she couldn't help but notice the difference in who I had become. "You were so uncertain of yourself and felt small and maybe a little lost?" She said, another friend chimed in "you feel SO YOU. Like *pow!* Ashley Adamson!" I was a bit surprised at the commentary not because I didn't already feel this way but because I had forgotten that I didn't always feel this way.

That's the thing about transformation. The change is so rapid you forget where you came from because you lose track of the iterations of the self.

When you're doing the deep work it's unclear where the work will take you. It can feel overwhelming, underwhelming, and a pain in the ass. Your confidence can feel shattered and others will see it. But at some point the hard parts just dissolve and you end up with all the jewels of your hard work.

The person I am now feels like I've always been this way because I have. However I spent 35 years going through the process of shaving off the layers of systemic, ideologic, and inherited bullshit.

I believe every human is a special being but most people don't put in the effort to uncover what lies beneath. And this is one of the greatest gifts in transitioning- it is the result of the process and the experience of going through complete inner and outer transformation.

At the end of the day, when you look back at your life, you'll know that you did the best thing for yourself. Do the deep work and others will feel it too, even if they're not conscious of it. Change yourself and the world will change around you. Authenticity has a way of being contagious.

Thought meditation:

You have a future self and in moments of transition it's a great practice to call on this future self to anchor a direction, feeling, and vision. With an idea of where you see yourself arriving you can then listen to your intuition and let it guide you towards your future self waiting for you at the other side.

At the very beginning of my transition I started to have visions of my future self. In one of those visions I saw a gorgeous photo of woman who, to my surprise, was me. I was standing on a mountain cliff looking out onto the world. The vision just rushed through me as I was walking back with my friend holding me. I stopped right there and said "Gosh I just saw my future self and she's a beautiful woman!. "How can this be?", I wondered. . It wasn't believable to my conscious mind at the time but I chose to believe in it. Throughout my ups and downs I remember anchoring myself on this original vision. It gave me hope. I have never seen that picture of me on a mountain but now that I am two and one half years later I can clearly see that I have arrived in that future self that I saw in the photo.

For this meditation:

- Envision an ideal outcome for your transition.

- What does it look like?

- How does it feel?

- Take a moment to soak up this feeling and anchor it into an image.

- Use this image as a way to remind yourself of where you will go. At times, if you feel lost or hopeless, return to this anchor and use it to call upon your vision, to remind yourself of your potential and where you can go.

What's at the core of a transition?

So those are all the major stages of a transition. But what's at the core of a transition? It's simple, it's you. Or is it?

When you're changing who you are you are changing the definition of "you." When you move through the process of transitioning you're continuing to change that definition. I remember how disorienting it was thinking I was one person one day and then the next day I felt totally different about who I was - that's fluidity. And there's fluidity in the process as we shed away the old self like the skin off a snake - except a snake doesn't shed skin everyday.

For most of us, we don't want the fluidity of our identity to be a constant focal point for the rest of our lives and so a part of transition is to find a foundation - a solid place to feel grounded and grow from.

At the heart of your transition is a
movement towards the center of who you
really are.

What that means is: a lot of your change is not about innovation of your character but about finding out the essence of who you really are and bringing that to the surface. This is your essential nature - when you get to the end of your transition you will see that you already are who you are. And ironically, you always have been. You may not like parts of who you are now and that's okay. With time you will learn to discard the parts that are not really your essence and hopefully shed the layers of falsities that hold you back from embracing and loving yourself.

To embody who you truly are, you will need to understand some fundamentals about how your world works.

Did you know you have two worlds?

"What do you mean? I thought there was only one world?" True, there is only one planet but there is also a completely separate world inside of you - your world. It's rich, complex, and the further you explore it the more infinite its depth appears.

The two worlds are:

- Your inner world: how you feel, how you perceive, and experience.

- Your outer world: the physical tangible world you can see and touch.

Understanding you exist in both is crucial to recognizing how the parts of your identity come together.

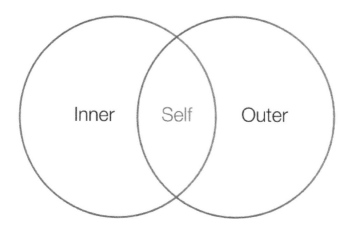

Inner Self Outer

When we draw these two worlds you will see they intersect and overlap. In the middle is your self. It is neither exclusively your inner world nor your outer world. The self being is the intersectional experience of the outer and inner worlds. To identity with one exclusively would be to miss the reality of who you actually are. You are more than your thoughts, you are more than your body.

Understanding these relationships between inner, outer, and self are crucial in working with yourself.

Living in the outer world

Understanding the outer world is easy. It's the world that physically exists. The one you can touch. When thinking about your transition this is about your body and how you physically exist in a world where others exist.

Being trans usually makes living in the outer world harder - but not impossible- because the way the outer world works is not usually supportive of your trans existence. Going out as your true self and coming out to others can be a scary thought… but it doesn't have to be.

The great thing about the external world is you can change it very quickly. If you want to look different you can change your appearance. If you want a glass of water you can go get it. Changing your external world can be easy. It takes physical effort, but not much more. Just do the thing and it can be done. There are limits too and I've struggled with this when it relates to changing my body. I can't blink and then change all the body parts to exactly what I want, but this is where self-acceptance comes into play.

Coming to terms with self acceptance is also learning to accept the things you cannot change and stopping comparing yourself to others who may have what you want. I know it's hard. I can't avoid it all the time, but do your best to not compare. Best to teach yourself through the habit of compassion to over continual dissatisfaction and not feeling "enough."

Putting the physically impossible aside, the outer world is the easier place to enact change because you can change it very quickly, it's up to you to decide the pace.

The inner world

The inner world is the place of your perceptual experience. It's where imagination plays, where you experience your experience and where your thoughts and feelings are seen and felt.

Mini-exercise:

Close your eyes for a moment and see where your thoughts are.

That is where you are - you are in your inner world right now.

Whatever you are perceiving, that is where you are in your inner world.

The great thing about the inner world is it's non-physical. Which means it's very malleable and can be molded to fit your needs. In any moment, given the right circumstances, you can become your true self.

Easier said than done, but in the right frame of mind you can be who you want to be - right now. It's all about figuring out the short cuts and ways to put you in a state to access it.

Actualizing your true self involves dissecting the inner and outer world you've identified with and piecing it back together again in a more honest and authentic way.

Your true self and shifting identity

Within these overlaps of the inner and outer world is the self.

It's important to note that your self is not your identity. Using the redecorating your room analogy, you may change the furniture and decorations in your room which is like changing your identity.

However, while the room looks and feels different it remains a room - the room is the self, the stuff in it is your identity. Being transgender and transitioning is aligning your identity with your self. Yet, the self is not transgender - that would dilute the full potential of who you truly are. Your self is more than your identity. More on this later. But first let's break down identity.

- Your identity is an attachment to an idea of who you *think* you are. It is composed of attachments from the inner and outer world.

- The identity is a construct of the ego. An accumulation of self-judgements and reflections intertwined with what intuitively feels like you.

- The identity works well most of the time because you have evolved it to not exist in conflict with who you are. Yet, when you transition you come into direct conflict by pitting your old identity with your new to-be identity.

- As you transition a lot of your pain will come from the destruction of your old identity and the birth of a new one.

- In this sense your identity will change and can be fluid, yet the self will not change. Just how you interpret it will be different.

- As you grow and change you may change as a person and you may identify differently but as long as you maintain a connection to this deeper sense of who you are you will always remain your true self.

- A strong attachment to identity makes you harder to change. Which is fine when you need it. But if you're in a transition then you may need to loosen your grasp on your identity.

- When you change you will eventually arrive at a new identity. This is great, it gives you a base to build from.

- Identity and ego should not be avoided but embraced as tools to help give you a sense of place of who you are in the world and form a base from which to stand in when you speak.

- The only time we need to let go of the ego/identity is when we need to move beyond what we know.

While your identity may change, the self remains - it is the room.

How you interpret the self will evolve as you learn and develop as a person but the mystical aspect of the self is that its essence is always there. Just waiting to be heard. I believe as we progress through life we are on a journey of continually unraveling the mystery of who we really are. To ask this question feels fundamental to the curiosity of being human.

Personally, I find that the self lives somewhere deeper within my heart. When I was dancing at a festival and I experienced my rebirth as "she" entering my body, I suddenly came in touch with the self. It felt like I experienced a "knowing" beyond cognitive understanding. I "just knew" that this was me, I was "her." If you keep asking me "Why am I woman?" ,eventually it comes down to

"I just know." It is beyond explanation. It is a static sense of being and that is my true self - it prefers to occupy a feminine space and in society that means being a woman.

Searching for your self can be disorienting at times but it's good to do self-inquiry and ask fundamental questions.

"Who am I? What am I?" I'd often ask myself these questions as I began to evolve through my transition. It felt like I was birthing a new being into existence that I didn't know. It was so unfamiliar yet as she emerged and settled it became clear I had just ignored her.

Finding your self involves sorting through these questions and detangling your identity with the things that are no longer true. This often means looking at how you've seen your outer world and inner world.

To draw more contrast between these worlds:

- If you identify with your outer world then you identify with your body, how you look, and what you've accomplished.

- If you identify into your inner world you begin to identify with the thoughts, feelings, and experiences you have. But you are not your thoughts.

So what are you? That is up to you to uncover and using your inner compass will help guide you through the unknown. More on the inner compass later.

Mini-exercise:

Close your eyes and imagine for a moment that you were to open a door to meet yourself without a physical body.

- How would they appear? That is your true self and how it wants to be seen right now.

- You can extend this exercise to imagining the door opening inside your heart and letting them out.

It's important to note that the self already knows who you are.

The inner world, outer world, and self are all intertwined in your experience and while it's good to identify them as distinct, in reality they feel interwoven.

Gender dysphoria is an example of how all these worlds meet. You see your body (the external world) does not match what you know about yourself (the self) and you (as the internal world) experience negative thoughts. If you identify with these thoughts then you experience suffering.

The most important distinction to be made here echoes the wisdom of mindfulness practitioners everywhere, which is: you are not your thoughts (internal) or your body (external). You are an experiencer of both (the self) and the more you can get on board with understanding that your internal world is not you, nor is your external world, then you'll be able to reduce suffering. If you'd like to go more in-depth with me you can come to one of my guided meditation groups or join a workshop I'll be hosting. More info on my website.

The more closely you identify with the state of your internal world - your thoughts and feelings, the more suffering you will endure. "I'm a fake," "I'll never be beautiful," or "I'll never be safe, or accepted" are thoughts that aren't objectively true but may feel true depending on how attached you are to experiencing them. I personally struggle with these thoughts now and then and I don't know if I will ever rid myself of them. It is a practice to be mindful of their existence and to not fight them but let them be and continue on. Left alone, these types of thoughts may fade into the background.

It's your relationship with these artifacts of the inner world (your thoughts and feelings) that influences your sense of well being. Your thoughts translate to feelings, assuming you give them your attention. Therefore, your ability to be freed from your negative thoughts and feelings is largely a function of your ability to un-believe them and to see yourself as an experiencer of the inner world but not become attached or identify with it. Be an observer.

Now that we've established the inner world, outer world, and the self we can talk about how we work with these three fundamental components to unlock your complete transgender transformation.

Side note:

Gender dysphoria is a tough nut to crack and we all have our issues. I recommend examining the why behind your perception and see if you can get to the root beliefs that construct your perception and in turn your judgement of what you see. For example, when I realized that many women also have broader shoulders that are wider than their hips then that changed my definition of what is female and helped me shift my perception of my own hip dysphoria.

Worlds influencing each other

Do you remember the last big thing you did yourself that made you truly euphoric? Euphoria is a great example of how you can get a reaction from both your inner and outer world by doing something that influences the other. Dressing up and feeling gender affirmed is a big one for most trans folks.

For me, the catalyzing moment was when I put on some makeup, a wig, and a mini-skirt to go clubbing with my girlfriends. Later that night, what I saw in the women's bathroom mirror shocked me. Who was that? I saw a woman. Was it me!? My outer world appearance had changed enough with the influence of the neuro chemical release in my brain to help me let go of my attachments to the inner/outer world I believe I existed in - a male in a male body. It gave me a moment for my true self and inner/outer world to see eye-to-eye for the first time, quite literally in the mirror.

That's an extreme example of how you can change your outer world to affect your inner world but there are many small things you can do too. Like wearing outfits that feel validating, changing your pronouns, mannerisms, voice, behavior, you name it!

Transitioning is a very personal thing and you don't need to take hormones or do anything to be trans, you just need to do what makes sense for you. I think a mental transition is probably the baseline. The important thing is to try these things and see what feels right to you.

Whatever you do to transition, just know that the outer world will take time to adjust to your changes. I see people take it very personally when they get misgendered, I get it. It hurts. But try not to take it personally when people honestly mess up. It's completely normal and somewhat expected that most people will have not done the deep inner work you are doing around your gender. Patience and time will help others evolve with you.

Now that we've covered the most important bit, let's talk about the tools that help you work with your inner and outer world.

A magic toolbox for transitioning

Transitioning is a beast of a project. It doesn't need to be difficult but it's best that you come prepared - equipped with the best knowledge, approach, strategy and tactics. Now that we've addressed the most fundamental parts of transformation - understanding the self, and the inner/outer worlds, let's get into more tangible things to approach making your transition as smooth and graceful as possible.

Bookmark and share this!

There are many tools to equip yourself with to move through your transition. Bookmark this page and come back to it later - there are a lot! We go into more detail on how to work with these in our workshop and live guided meditation series.

If you'd like to go more in-depth with me you can come to one of my guided meditation groups or join a workshop I'll be hosting. More info on my website.

Your strategy is building resilience

Transitioning when you're at your best feels great but the lows in a transition can go very low and who's going to catch you when you're down? This is where resilience comes into play, and it's the most important skill to develop to get up when you're down and keep moving forward.

Resiliency is where you will find your greatest strength and the internal work is a huge component of that. Below we'll go into some key personal growth concepts and practices that will help you build resilience.

Unlocking self acceptance

Aka accepting yourself. Self-acceptance is probably the most important internal practice to work on when building up your resilience. If you can stop struggling with yourself then you can make decisions from a place that enables you to step forward into your life and build a better one.

Self-acceptance. Simple word, but not always so simple. When you break this concept down it exists in many layers. Accepting yourself is a process and it takes time and effort to recalibrate your own beliefs of yourself and what is "acceptable" and who can give you love - including yourself.

I've found that the secret to self-love is undoing the belief that only others can give you love, and that you are just as valid to give love to yourself. Loving yourself means loving parts of yourself you dislike or even hate. Until everything of the self is embraced, you will find self-love a more elusive practice.

Finding self-acceptance is not an achievement to be perfected. At times you can be thrown off, get frustrated or dislike something about yourself. But in these moments it's about finding the strength and compassion to take a step back from the emotionally loaded experience that set you off so you can come back to a sense of self-acceptance.

Here are a few areas and practices that can help build more self-acceptance.

Letting go

Imagine holding a ball, now let it go. Easy to do when the ball is physical. Now imagine letting go of your arm. Not so easy. Letting go is one of the things I've struggled with the most. It's just hard to say goodbye to things that you love, even if they're no longer good for you. The more invested you are in something the harder it is to let go, our identities are just so wrapped up in them. When it comes to who you see in the mirror, who you think you are, and how you see your trans identity these are all things that we hold very close. Letting them go can be very painful. Through my own process and sharing with other trans people I've coached, I find the best way to describe the feeling is you're burning it down. That old identity has to go in order to make room for the new one.

Thought meditation: Take a moment to close your eyes and hold your hand closed like you're holding onto something. Imagine that thing your holding onto is an aspect of your identity. Then slowly practice letting go by physically letting go. Watch and see how you respond to this sensation of letting go.

Self love is not some mystical magical unicorn

Self love is not something that only the few self-help gurus can give you. Self love is just the art of practicing self love. Loving yourself really just means acknowledging the different parts of yourself, even the "ugly" ones that you may judge and not accept and bringing them into the fold of your embrace. My first experience with self-love came when I was able to distinguish all the parts of me that I didn't accept or like and visualize hugging all of them with all the love I could give. The final step for me was to unbind my belief from the idea that love is something other people give to other people. I think the idea of love as an external source is a deep seeded belief in our society because we learn what love is from others and so we believe it must come from one to another. Yet, detangling this connection of relying on an external source really helped me find a way to love myself more.

Practices:

1. Mini practice: Add a little post-it on the mirror that affirms that you love yourself and repeat it every time you look in the mirror. Sounded dumb to me, but worked great!

2. Deep practice: Take a moment to reflect on all the parts of you that you

know of. Write them down and label them with names. Now take a moment to imagine all of them within you and give them a biiiiiig hug! 🫂

When you're drained it's best to get a little self-care in

Having a hard time? When the going gets tough you're going to need to have a backup plan for supporting yourself when you are exhausted or feel like you've fallen down. So it's okay to take breaks and do things to get your mind off things if it feels like a struggle.

Practices:

- I love taking baths, hot showers, playing games, writing or going dancing. Do something that is an act of care to yourself. You need to remember to fill your cup.

Thought Exercise:

- What's something you enjoy doing for yourself that you don't do often? Go do it!

Learning To Use Your Inner Compass when faced with the Unknown

Your inner compass is probably the most important tool you can use in navigating through the unknown. The unknown is like a black box - full of possibility, which is exciting but also frightening. How do you move through the dark into the unknown when you don't know the path forward? That's where your inner compass comes in and learning how to read the signals will be instrumental in helping you make better decisions that lead to a graceful transition.

To listen to your inner compass all you need to do is set your intention to check in and listen.

Every inner compass will manifest differently

depending on how you like to receive signs. Setting the intent to ask your compass questions is how you start. Think of it like developing a skill, the more you practice the better you'll get. Some people describe the feeling as "just feels right." And it shows up like that for me too. Here's an example concerning discovering my sexuality.

I had dated exclusively women my entire life and transitioned with another woman until things ended. Till that point I had been a hetero male and then a trans lesbian but I was curious to date a man as I had a feeling I *might* like it. It was on my second date with the first man I ever dated that I felt my inner compass speak loudly.

It was a rainy night in San Francisco and we had just had dinner. As we left the restaurant he held me close through the cold as we walked through the rain under his umbrella. He was bigger than me and I felt so safe and cared for. He opened the door to his car like a gentleman and we drove off to the metropolitan museum. With the raindrops pattering on the windshield, I leaned over and held his hand. A rush crept through me. Life was so wonderful, as if everything settled into place. I suddenly realized I had been seeking this balance my entire life in my relationships with women but I could not access it as a man. My heart pounded a little bit and it just felt so right. So this is it?I thought. I actually prefer men?

As time has progressed I've attuned myself to the feeling of the inner compass and I use it often in my transition as a temperature check to see if I'm missing something or if I'm doing the right thing. It shows up unexpectedly when I try new things like in the example of the date, but at the same time it pushed me to try out that date in the first place because I had a *feeling*.

Where do you have a *feeling* of something you should try or do? Can you do it?

When I want to check in with my compass I may ask myself: "What do I know about _____ that I am not consciously aware of?" Then I listen. It comes back not as a thought but as a feeling in my heart which gives me a sense of direction.

Sometimes, even if you know the direction you are headed is right you can feel like you're not getting anywhere.

Forming positive habits and finding consistency

The more you apply effort to self-acceptance the more you'll get out of it. The little post-it note trick above? Very little effort, but also very good for triggering the effort when you forget. The effect of doing things to improve your self-acceptance pays off in the long run. After a few weeks of using just the post-it note I noticed a shift in my perception.

Your efforts compound the more consistently you do it. Don't just save self-acceptance for the end of the week. Do it every day, big or small it doesn't matter so long as you keep yourself moving.

Transitioning and finding self acceptance isn't just about confronting your inner demons. It's also about creating positive foundational habits that will help your mind and body naturally grow and adjust to a new paradigm. Positive habits are at the crux of any personal growth regime and for good reason. They do good things for you. If you do something that makes you happier, healthier, and feeling more free you'll have better mental capacity to handle the complexities of redoing yourself.

Exercise: What can you do for yourself that would be an act of self-care or practicing self-acceptance? What's one little thing you can do to help ground your intentions for the day? Can you bring yourself back to this intention at some point later in the day? Do it!

Small habits are the best place to start though it can be hard to keep it up if you forget to do it. Try putting a new habit somewhere where you already have a habit. Like waking up or going to bed - tag on the new positive habit. Some simple positive habits can be doing a short prayer, meditation or reflection on being grateful.

Find your community, seek out social acceptance

Many times I have had moments where I felt like there was a deep pain in my heart I could not escape that crushed all my hopes, dreams and aspirations. Life has felt hopeless at times and I have questioned even going on with it. In these moments you need something to take care of yourself when you cannot find anyone else to help you.

As an operator on trans life line, the people I heard from who were struggling the most had no one to talk to about the issues surrounding them. They were alone and without guidance from even a single friend. It cannot be understated how important and valuable it is to have social contact and support from others who can give you a hug - even virtually to hear you out. You can find local communities or online communities like on Reddit, Discord, or my Youtube.

Exercise:

How do you like to be supported? Make a list of people you think might be able to help you with some of these areas. Give them a call, text them, meet up check in with them to support them and also ask for their support in whatever way feels comfortable. Establishing a connection by paying it forward will give dividends later when you really need it.

Practicing patience when you feel like you're not getting anywhere

Whenever you feel like you're stuck it might be worth a second to take a step back and reflect on a few things. Bookmark this piece because you'll need to read it when you feel stuck.

1. Look how far you've come. In the heat of the moment you can be selective in what you think progress is. We humans have a recency bias to see things as of recently rather than take in the bigger narrative arc of our lives. Take a second to reflect on how far you've

come, even pre-transition. All of it has lead you to this point. You've survived! And you have so much more life to live as your new self.

2. It takes time for the world to align. Your life is like a giant boat going in a direction built off of the momentum of your previous events and decisions. When you start making radical changes to your life it takes a while for your world to align with you. As your outer world soon aligns with your inner world the feedback effect of the outer world, such as people gendering you correctly, has an effect on your internal world.

3. Our brains are slow to adjust. It just takes time for our brains to adjust.

Even if you can consciously be aware of your true self you still have ingrained thought patterns and behaviors that can derail you from time to time. Dealing with personal issues and overcoming them happens like peeling back layers of an onion. What was it like the first time you confronted yourself about being trans? You may have not accepted you were trans but over time you peeled back those layers of resistance so you could have a proper dialogue about it. Self-acceptance is multi-faceted and takes time to peel back the layers of doubt, resistance, and denial. The important thing is to try to be consistent and patient with your brain and how you care for yourself.

Doubt

Another key holder in unlocking our true self. Having doubt is not a bad thing - it does allow us to have some filtration of information we receive and be inquisitive and skeptical. Where I see it gets in the way most for trans people is they doubt the decisions they are making, saying "It's just a phase" or "I'll never achieve [x]" or "I'll never pass" or something like that. I've had those thoughts and gone through many stages of doubt. To be honest, I still have doubt come up every now and then but it's a lot easier to shrug off.

The best thing to do with doubt is to dispel its credibility and not feed it your energy. Doubt often doesn't make a lot of sense and when you start to examine the logic it falls flat pretty quickly. The thing is - most of the time we never consciously engage with doubt. What's the first thing you do when you hear a doubtful voice? You try to push it away, right?

Trying to push away negative thoughts can work in the short term but it still requires energy to hold it back. The more you hold it back the more power you give it to exist.

Exercise: Take a moment to write down on a piece of paper some of the thoughts that you have that doubt you. Ask "Well why is that true?" or "What's the worst that would happen?" and keep asking those questions until you get to the end of the logic tree. You'll see that none of them really have any grounding in your day-to-day reality.

Resistance

"Why am I resisting this change?" I asked myself this a lot even a year after I began my transition. Once you clean out the big monsters in your consciousness that are holding you back you'll soon find small nooks and crannies of resistance to change. Here's where the practice of letting go can really help you stop resisting.

Exercise: It's important to also create a dialogue with your resistance. Try noticing when you are resisting something and ask yourself. "Why am I resisting?" "What is so important that I resist this concept that I know will help me?" "What am I afraid of?" "What's the worst that could happen?"

Denial

Denial is a tricky one, it's one of the first layers you'll have to come up against before doubt. You can doubt something so much that you'll just deny its existence in your conscious mind.

I discovered my own denial when I realized that to me the idea of transitioning was such a serious topic and the stakes so high that the perceived danger was too great for me to even consider I was trans. Combine that with the trans narrative not matching the one that is perpetuated - "I always knew I was trans." I just didn't think I could consider that I too was also trans.

Denial is kind of an escape in a way. It lets you put something aside that you don't want to or are not ready to process. That's fine too, sometimes we just cannot process too much at the same time and denial is a great tactic for the mind to help us cope. But when will you come back to addressing the hard stuff? When will you have space to look and ask yourself the harder questions?

I found my process of transitioning to be intertwined with layer after layer of denial. First it was denial that I was trans. Then it was denial that I was a trans woman - I started out thinking I might be gender fluid, and then it was denial that I could embody femininity. Those are the major milestones of denial for me and I was able to address each one as I took steps forward to feel ready to cope with it.

Denial works with big emotionally loaded topics and the weight of processing it can feel too great at times. I get that. What I've found to be more helpful is to actually de-escalate the perceived burden of the issue. To actually take the BIG thing and make it small. Don't try to chew the big topic of whatever you want to go through but chew away at a smaller aspect of it.

One of my favorite ways to work with denial is to introduce exploratory play. Make it a smaller thing to experiment and try and work with. For example, dressing up to me as a woman was "just experimenting" and for fun but not for anything serious except exploration. When I had done enough exploring, I could finally take the big question of "Am I woman?" off the shelf and see it for what it was.

Thought meditation: What's a big area you think you're in denial of? What is a small way you can nudge up against the topic? Is there a way you could be playful with it? Make it an experiment? Try framing a small activity on the topic as "just an experiment" and go for it. Don't expect any outcome or project what you think might happen when you do the activity. Just remain open to exploring and see what comes up. What can you learn from this?

Stop Being So Damn Mean to Yourself

I don't know about you but my expectations for myself are often higher than my expectations of other people. If I'm not doing something well I can feel flustered or even upset because something is not going my way. Change might not be happening at the pace I want it to or something I thought I got over comes back up to bite me. In these moments it's important to take a step back and realize you're doing a lot of deep work. This is a hard process and there aren't a lot of guides on how to do this (except this one lol).

Exercise: Give yourself a pat on the back for the things you've done right today. Take a bigger perspective and look at the story arch of the last year. You've probably done a lot more than you give yourself credit for.

Dysphoria coping strategies

I hate dysphoria, you hate it. I think it's the bane of all trans people's experience. While dysphoria takes a long time to heal or may even feel permanent we can develop habits, ways of seeing things, and tactics to push back on the little voice that makes us believe we're not valid in our bodies. You'll learn how to fight back over time and it will become less of a problem as you take steps to heal yourself. Here are a few things that have worked for me.

- Taking photos and picking out the best ones of myself.

- Preparing myself before I look into the mirror to program my instincts to see a girl.

- Putting the I am beautiful post-it on my wall.

- Spending money on gender affirming clothes.

- Spending money on gender affirming surgery.

- Asking others people's opinions to get out of my own story, the story of what I see.

- Learning to let go of the idea that my body needs to be a "perfect image" of a woman's body and recognize that other women don't have it or need it.

- Catching myself when I'm selectively comparing myself to other women. You have to take in the whole picture of women's bodies for example. There's many types!

- Dating people who see me in the way I want to see myself. They see me as attractive and that makes me feel attractive!

- Complementing my body.

- Taking care of it and exercising to make my body look even better!

Exercises:

Try out some of the things listed above or invent your own. I think you have an idea of what you can do now!

What's next?

You may join me for guided inner work sessions and ongoing groups I am moderating. If you're interested in one of these programs reach out ashleyxadamson@gmail.com or visit my www.ashleyxadamson.com.

I encourage you to re-read this at different stages of your transition. There is deep meaning encoded and depending at what level your processing different things will click. Maybe come back once every three months. Every section could be written into it's own book but I tried to keep it light yet dense. I suggest you bookmark this and please help me by sharing it with your friends. As you evolve you will probably come to a new understanding of what was conveyed in here.

If you'd like to go more in-depth with me you can come to one of my guided meditation groups or join a workshop I'll be hosting. More info on my website.

Meet the Author

My name is Ashley Adamson and I'm a YouTuber and writer on transgender mindfulness, spirituality, and personal growth topics. I was inspired by working at Trans Lifeline to find a way to scale my efforts in supporting the trans community. I have appeared on MTV and spoken at Oxfam as well as numerous corporations, universities, and conferences.

You can find me on YouTube (https://www.youtube.com/ashleyxadamson) or on website (http://ashleyxadamson.com) .

Thank You!!!

I wanted to commemorate this book to all the people who were pivotal to my transition. It's been a long time coming and completing this adds finality to this stage in my own transition. For others reading this, it takes a village to raise a child. I was very lost at times and when I couldn't handle it on my own it was the power of family, friendship, and community that helped raise me up beyond anything I could of imagined.

My Family: Helyne, Jacquie, Lilly, John, Ewen.

My Teachers and Friends: Kip, Pat, Melina, Alan, Franni, Duncan

My Community Soul Tribe, Tokyo Alone Crew

My lovers You know who you are ;)

I want to write my own version of a book like this...

Made in the USA
Coppell, TX
04 December 2021

67078116R00080